TAYLOR SWIFT 1989

ISBN 978-1-4950-1100-9

HAL•LEONARD® CORPORATION

7777 W. BLUEMOUND RD. P.O. BOX 13819 MILWAUKEE, WI 53213

Visit Hal Leonard Online at
www.halleonard.com

Welcome to New York

Words and Music by Taylor Swift and Ryan Tedder

First note

Verse
Moderate Pop

N.C. (G)   (Dsus4)   (Csus2)

1. Walk - ing through a crowd, the Vil - lage is a - glow, ka -

(G)   (Dsus4)   (Csus2)   (G)   (Dsus4)

lei - do - scope of loud heart - beats un - der coats.   Ev - 'ry - bod - y here want - ed

(Csus2)   (G)   (Dsus4)   (Csus2)

some - thing more,   search - ing for a sound we had - n't heard be - fore.   And it said:

𝄋 Chorus

G   Dsus4   Csus2

Wel - come to New York,   it's been wait - ing for you.

G   Dsus4   Csus2   G   Dsus4   Csus2

Wel - come to New York, wel - come to New York.   Wel - come to New York,

it's been wait-ing for you. Wel-come to New York, wel-come

to New York. It's a new sound-track, I could dance to this

beat, _____ beat _____ for-ev-er-more. The lights are so ___

bright, but they nev-er blind me; _____ me. _____

Wel-come to New York, it's been wait-ing for you.

Wel-come to New York, wel-come to New York. *(claps)* 2. When

Verse

we first dropped our bags on a - part - ment floors,

took our bro - ken hearts, put them in a drawer.

Ev - 'ry - bod - y here was some - one else be - fore, and you can

watch who you want, boys and boys and girls and girls.

Coda
Bridge

Like an - y great love, it keeps you guess - ing.

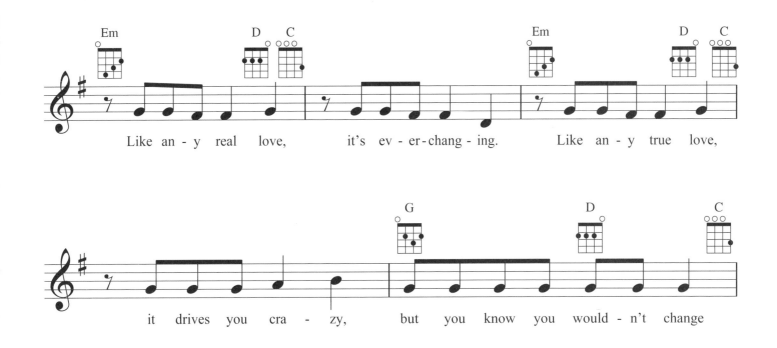

Like an - y real love, it's ev - er - chang - ing. Like an - y true love,

it drives you cra - zy, but you know you would - n't change

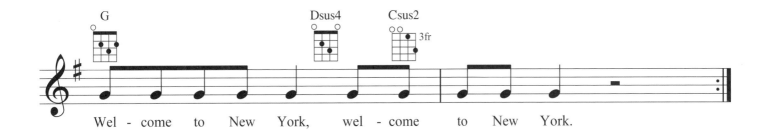

an - y - thing, an - y - thing, an - y - thing. _____

Chorus

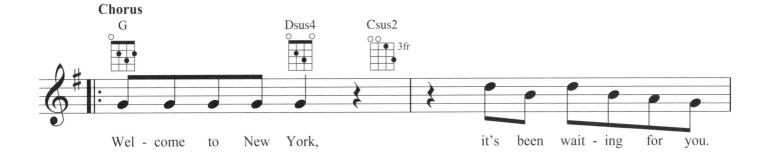

Wel - come to New York, it's been wait - ing for you.

Wel - come to New York, wel - come to New York.

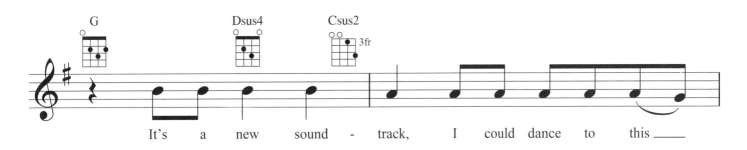

It's a new sound - track, I could dance to this ___

Out of the Woods

Words and Music by Taylor Swift and Jack Antonoff

-ered ___ (then dis-cov - ered) ___ the rest of the world was black and white ___

but we were in scream - ing col - or. ___ And I re-mem-ber think - ing:

𝄋 **Chorus**

Are we out of the woods ___ yet? Are we out of the woods _

___ yet? Are we out of the woods ___ yet? Are we out of the woods? _

___ Are we in the clear ___ yet? Are we in the clear _

___ yet? Are we in the clear ___ yet, in the clear ___ yet?

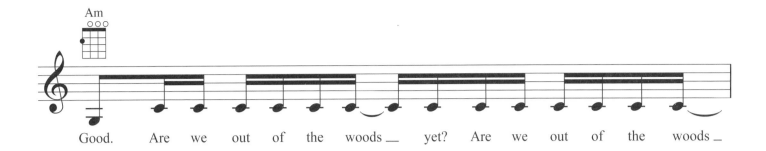

Good. Are we out of the woods __ yet? Are we out of the woods __

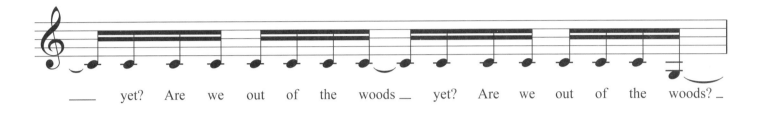

__ yet? Are we out of the woods __ yet? Are we out of the woods? __

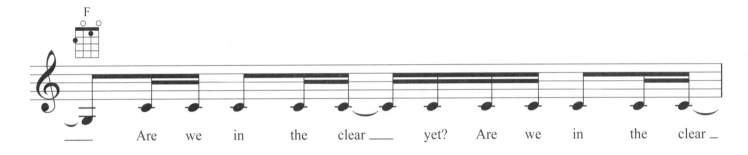

__ Are we in the clear __ yet? Are we in the clear __

__ yet? Are we in the clear __ yet, in the clear yet?

Good. (Oh, _____ oh.) _____ Are we out of the woods? _____

2. Look - ing at it now, _____ last De - cem -

-ber, _____ (last De-cem - ber,) _____ we were built to fall a-part, _____

then fall back to-geth - er, _____ (back to-geth -

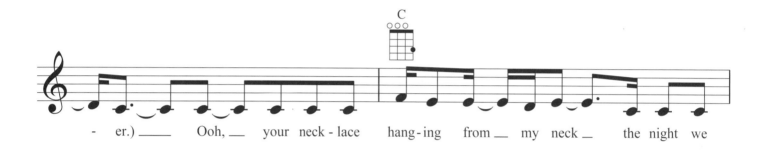

- er.) _____ Ooh, _____ your neck-lace hang-ing from _____ my neck _____ the night we

could-n't quite _____ for-get, _____ when we de-cid - ed, we de-cid -

- ed to move the fur - ni - ture _____ so we can dance, _____ ba - by,

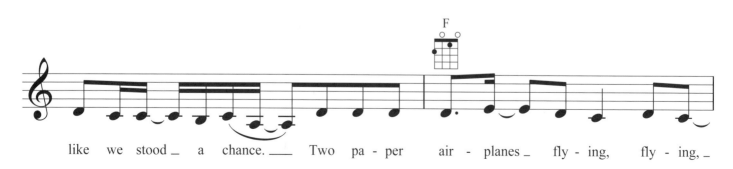

like we stood _____ a chance. _____ Two pa-per air - planes _____ fly - ing, fly - ing, _____

Interlude

you were look-ing at me. _____ (Are we out of the woods _ yet? Are we out of the woods _

_____ yet? Are we out of the woods _____ yet? Are we out of the woods? _ I re-mem-

- ber. _____ Are we in the clear _____ yet? Are we in the clear _____

_____ yet? Are we in...) Oh, I re-mem-ber.

Chorus

C

Are we out of the woods _____ yet? Are we out of the woods _

_____ yet? Are we out of the woods _____ yet? Are we out of the woods? _

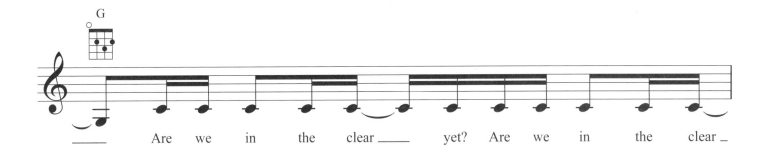

G

Are we in the clear ____ yet? Are we in the clear _

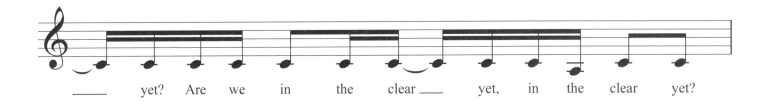

____ yet? Are we in the clear ____ yet, in the clear yet?

Am

Good. Are we out of the woods _ yet? Are we out of the woods _

___ yet? Are we out of the woods _ yet? Are we out of the woods? _

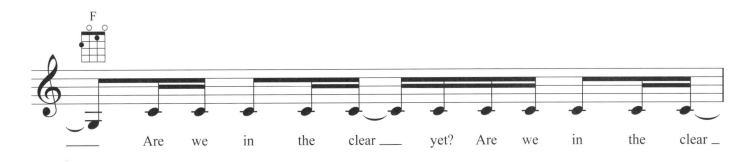

F

Are we in the clear ____ yet? Are we in the clear _

N.C.

____ yet? Are we in the clear _ yet, in the clear yet? Good.

Blank Space

Words and Music by Taylor Swift, Max Martin and Shellback

1. Nice to meet you; where you been? I could show _ you in-cred-i-ble
2. Cher-ry lips, _ crys-tal skies; I could show _ you in-cred-i-ble

things: _ mag-ic, mad-ness, heav-en, sin. Saw you there _ and I _____ thought,
things: _ sto-len kiss-es, pret-ty lies. You're the king, _ ba-by, I'm your

"Oh my God, look at that face! You look like my next mis-take.
queen. Find out what you want, be that girl for a month.

Love's a game; wan-na play?" _____ Eh.
Wait, the worst is yet to come. _____ Oh, _____ no.

New mon-ey, suit and tie; I can read __ you like a mag-a-
Scream-ing, cry-ing, per-fect storms; I can make __ all __ the ta - bles

zine. __ Ain't it fun-ny? Ru-mors fly, and I know __ you heard __ a-bout
turn. __ Rose __ gar-den filled with thorns; keep you sec - ond-guess-ing like,

me. So hey, let's be friends. I'm dy-ing to see how this one ends.
"Oh my God, who is she?" I ____ get drunk on jeal-ous-y. But

C   N.C.

Grab your pass-port and my hand. I can make the bad guys good for a week-end.
you'll come back __ each time you leave, 'cause, dar-ling, I'm a night-mare dressed like a day-dream.

𝄋 Chorus

So it's gon-na be for-ev-er, or it's gon-na go down in flames. __

Style

Words and Music by Taylor Swift, Max Martin, Shellback and Ali Payami

Pre-Chorus

Dm7

heard from you. ___
oth - er girl." ___

And I should just tell you to leave 'cause I
He says, "What you've heard is true, but I

Em7   Fmaj7 5fr

know ex - act - ly where it leads, but I
can't stop think - ing a - bout you and I."

watch us go 'round and 'round ___ each time. ___
I said, "I've been there too ___ a few

Chorus

C   G

times." ___
You got that James Dean day - dream look in your eye ___ and I got that

F   G

red lip, clas - sic thing that you ___ like. ___ And when we go

C   G

crash - ing down, we come back ev - 'ry time ___ 'cause we nev - er go

F   G

out of ___ style, ___ we nev - er go out of ___ style. ___ You got that

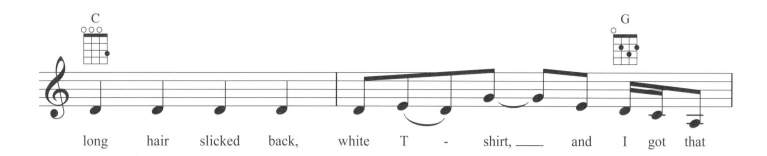

long hair slicked back, white T - shirt, ___ and I got that

good girl thing and a tight lit - tle ___ skirt. ___ And when we go

crash - ing down, we come back ev - 'ry time ___ 'cause we nev - er go

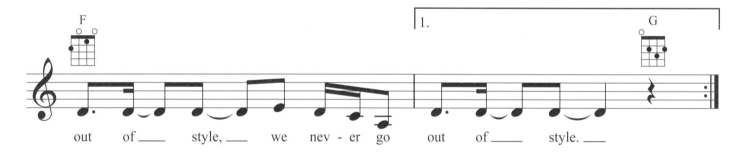

1.   G

out of ___ style, ___ we nev - er go out of ___ style. ___

2.   **Bridge**

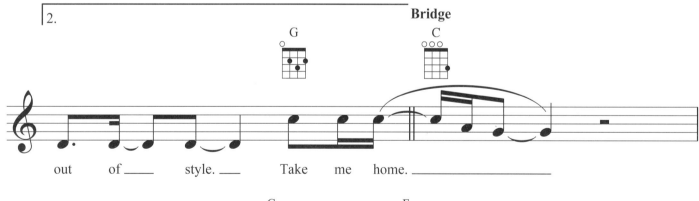

out of ___ style. ___ Take me home. _____

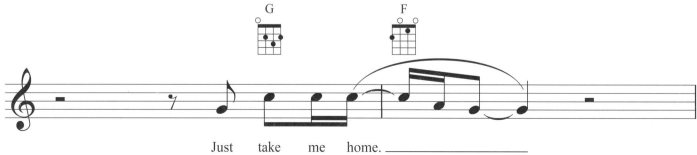

Just take me home. _____

Yeah, ___ just take me home. _____ Oh. _____

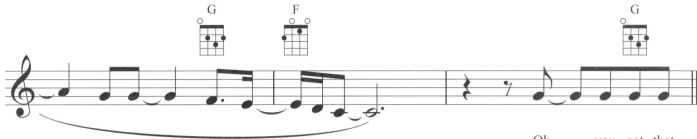

_____

Oh, ___ you got that

Outro-Chorus

James ___ Dean day - dream look in your ___ eye ___ and I got that

red lip, clas - sic thing that you ___ like. ___ And when we go

crash - ing down, we come back ev - 'ry time ___ 'cause we nev - er go

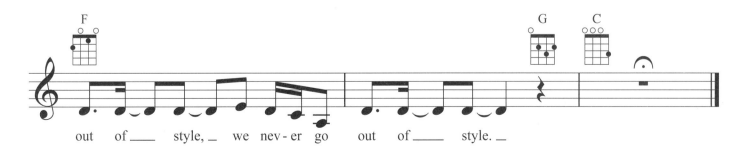

out of ___ style, _ we nev - er go out of ___ style. _

All You Had to Do Was Stay

Words and Music by Taylor Swift and Max Martin

Chorus

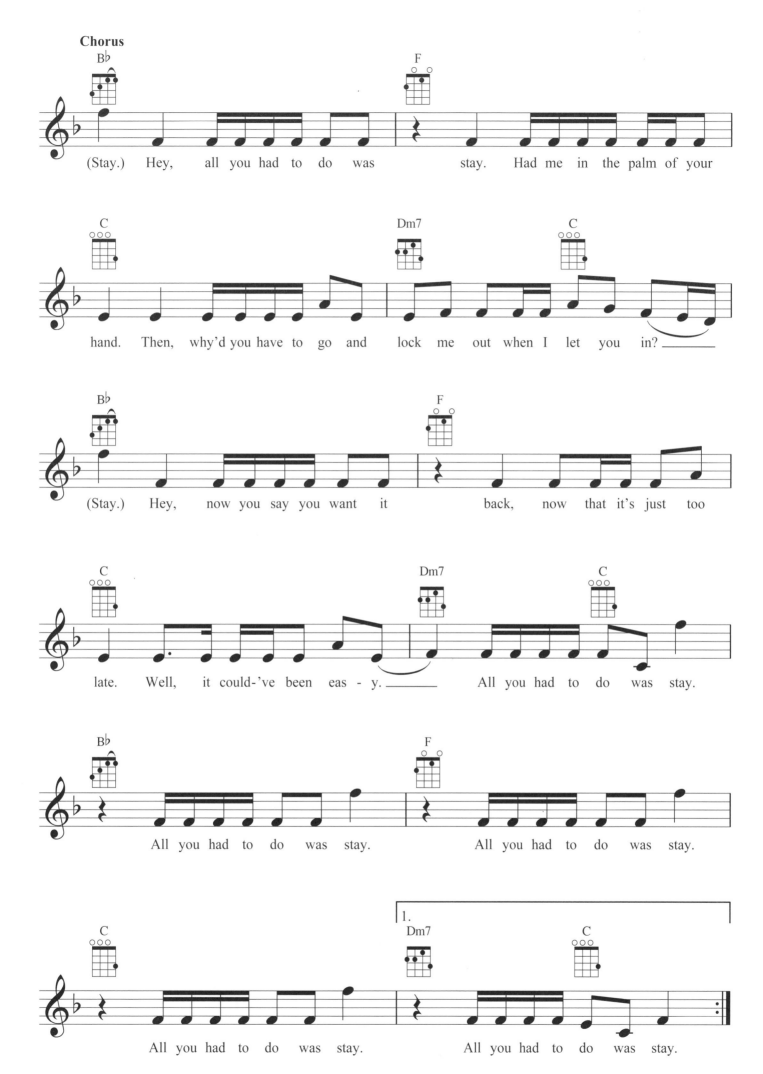

(Stay.) Hey, all you had to do was stay. Had me in the palm of your hand. Then, why'd you have to go and lock me out when I let you in? _____ (Stay.) Hey, now you say you want it back, now that it's just too late. Well, it could-'ve been eas - y. _____ All you had to do was stay. All you had to do was stay. All you had to do was stay.

1.

All you had to do was stay. All you had to do was stay.

Shake It Off

Words and Music by Taylor Swift, Max Martin and Shellback

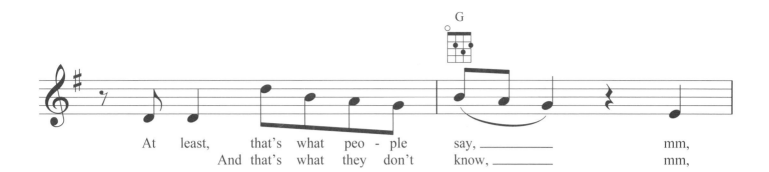

At least, that's what peo - ple say, _____ mm,
And that's what they don't know, _____ mm,

mm. That's what peo - ple say, _____ mm, mm. But I keep
mm. That's what they don't know, _____ mm, mm. But I keep

Pre-Chorus

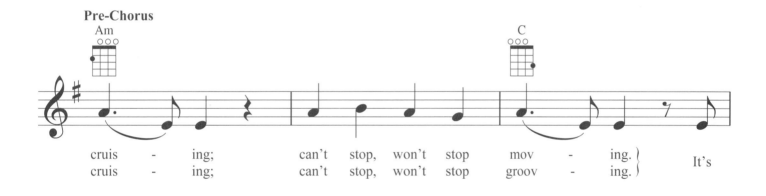

cruis - ing; can't stop, won't stop mov - ing. } It's
cruis - ing; can't stop, won't stop groov - ing. }

like I got this mu - sic in my mind say - ing,

"It's gon - na be al - right." _____ 'Cause the

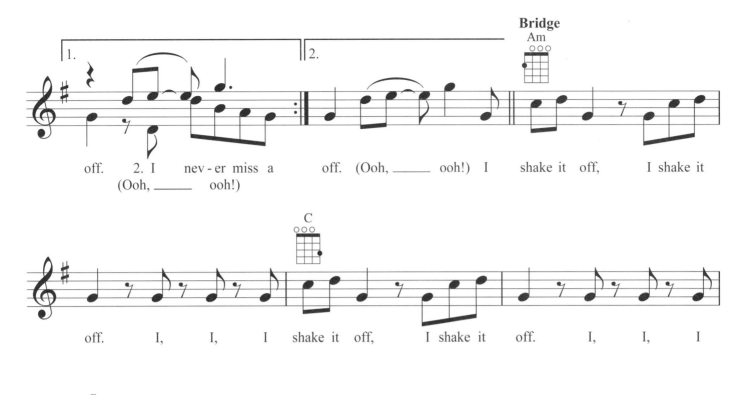

off.   2. I nev - er miss a   off. (Ooh, _____ ooh!) I   shake it off,   I shake it
(Ooh, _____ ooh!)

off. I,   I,   I shake it off,   I shake it   off.   I,   I,   I

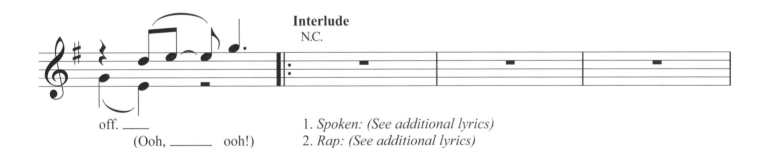

shake it off,   I shake it   off.   I,   I,   I   shake it off,   I shake it

Interlude

off. ____
(Ooh, _____ ooh!)

1. *Spoken: (See additional lyrics)*
2. *Rap: (See additional lyrics)*

D.S. al Coda

Rap ends   Yeah, _____ oh. _____ 'Cause the

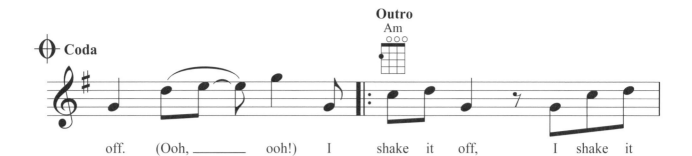

off. (Ooh, _____ ooh!) I shake it off, I shake it

off. I, I, I shake it off, I shake it off. I, I, I

shake it off, I shake it off. I, I, I shake it off, I shake it

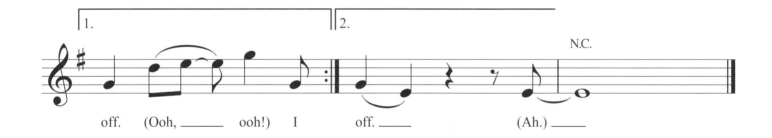

off. (Ooh, _____ ooh!) I off. _____ (Ah.) _____

Additional Lyrics

Spoken: Hey, hey, hey! Just think: While you've been gettin'
Down and out about the liars and the dirty, dirty cheats of the world,
You could've been gettin' down to this sick beat!

Rap: My ex-man brought his new girlfriend.
She's like, "Oh, my god!" But I'm just gonna shake.
And to the fella over there with the hella good hair,
Won't you come on over, baby? We can shake, shake, shake.

Bad Blood

Words and Music by Taylor Swift, Max Martin and Shellback

Pre-Chorus

Oh, it's so ____ sad ____ to

think a - bout ____ the good ____ times,

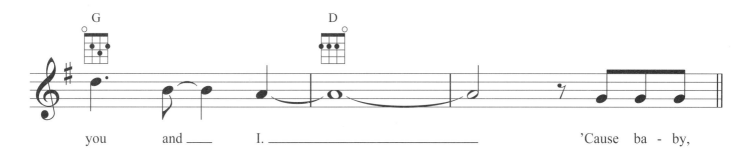

you and ____ I. ____ 'Cause ba - by,

Chorus

now we got bad ____ blood. You know it used to be mad ____

love. So take a look what you've done, ____ 'cause ba - by,

now we got bad ____ blood. Hey! Now we got prob -

*** Vocal sung at written pitch.*

lems, and I don't think we can solve _____ them. You made a

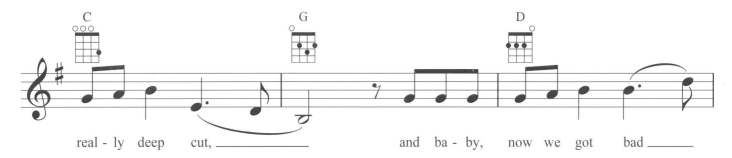

real - ly deep cut, _____ and ba - by, now we got bad _____

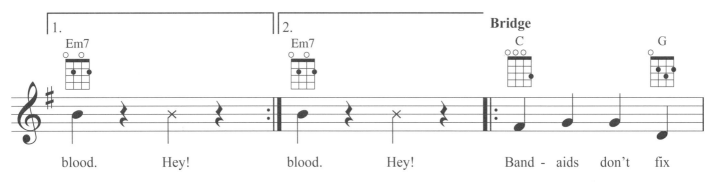

blood. Hey! blood. Hey! Band - aids don't fix

bul - let holes. _ You say sor - ry just for show. _ If you

live like that, you live with ghosts. _

Mm, _____ if you love _ like _ that, _

I Wish You Would

Words and Music by Taylor Swift and Jack Antonoff

wish you knew that I'll nev-er for-get ___ you as long ___ as I live. And I

wish you were right here, right now, it's all good. I wish you would. ___

___ I wish ___ we could go back and re-mem-ber what we were fight - ing for. And I

wish you knew that I miss you too much ___ to be mad ___ an-y-more. And I

To Coda ⊕

wish you were right here, right now, it's all good. I wish you would. ___

Interlude

___ (I, I, I, ___ I, I, I wish, I wish, I. I, I, I, ___ I,

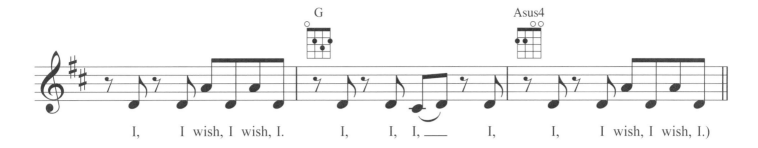

I, I wish, I wish, I.   I, I, I,___ I, I, I wish, I wish, I.)

Bridge

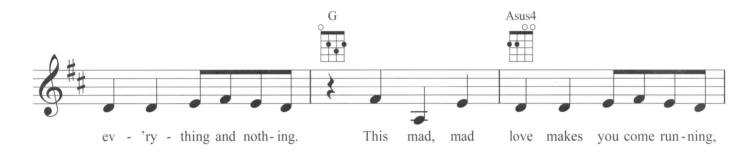

You al - ways knew how to push my but - tons. You give me

ev - 'ry - thing and noth - ing. This mad, mad love makes you come run - ning,

to stand back where you stood, ___ I wish you would, _ I wish you would. _

___ I wish you would, _ I wish you would. _____ (I,

Verse

I, I wish, I wish, I.)   3. Two a. m., here we are,

knew how to push my but - tons. You give me ev - 'ry - thing and noth - ing.

This mad, mad love makes you come run - ning, to stand back where you stood, _

_ I wish you would, _ I wish you would. _____

I wish you would, _ I wish you would. _____ (I,

Outro

I, I wish, I wish, I. I, I, I, _ I, I, I wish, I wish, I.

I, I, I, _ I, I, I wish.) I wish you would. _

Wildest Dreams

Words and Music by Taylor Swift, Max Martin and Shellback

does it so __ well. ____ I can see the end as it be - gins, my
does it so __ well. ____ And when we've had our ver - y last kiss, my

𝄉 **Chorus**

one con - di - tion is: __ Say you'll re - mem - ber me ____ stand - ing in a
last re - quest _ is: __

nice dress, star - ing at the sun - set, babe. Red lips and ros - y cheeks, _

__ say you'll see me a - gain, e - ven if it's just in your

wild - est dreams, _____ ah, _____ ah. _____

To Coda ⊕

Wild - est dreams, _____ ah, _____

Red lips and ros - y cheeks, __ say you'll see me a - gain, e - ven if it's

D.S. al Coda

⊕ **Coda** E♭

just pre - tend.

In your

Outro

wild - est dreams, _____ ah, _____ ah. _____ E - ven if it's

just in your... _____
In your wild - est dreams, _____ ah, _____

ah. _____ In _____ your wild - est dreams, __

_____ _____ ah, _____ ah. _____

How You Get the Girl

Words and Music by Taylor Swift, Max Martin and Shellback

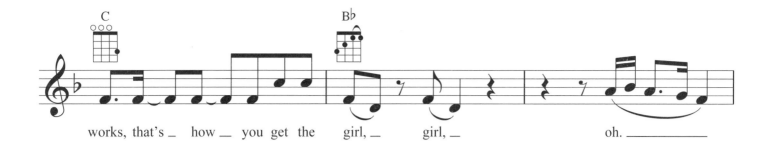

works, that's how you get the girl, girl, oh.

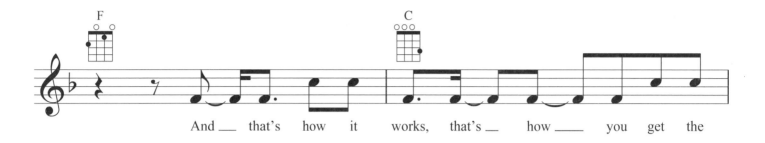

And that's how it works, that's how you get the

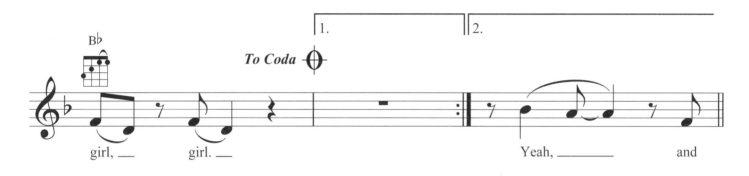

To Coda

1. girl, girl.

2. Yeah, and

Bridge

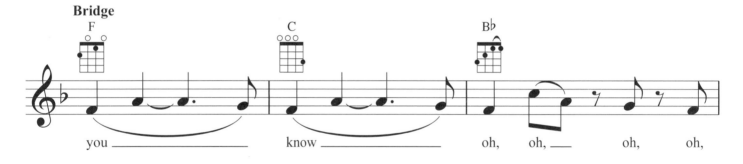

you know oh, oh, oh, oh,

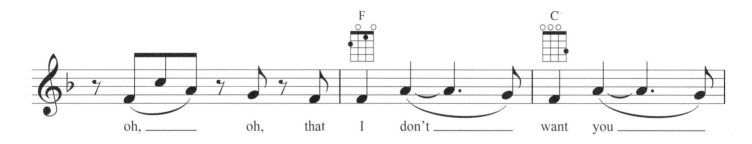

oh, oh, that I don't want you

Pre-Chorus

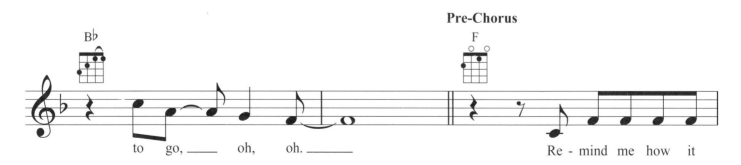

to go, oh, oh. Re - mind me how it

This Love

Words and Music by Taylor Swift

I Know Places

Words and Music by Taylor Swift and Ryan Tedder

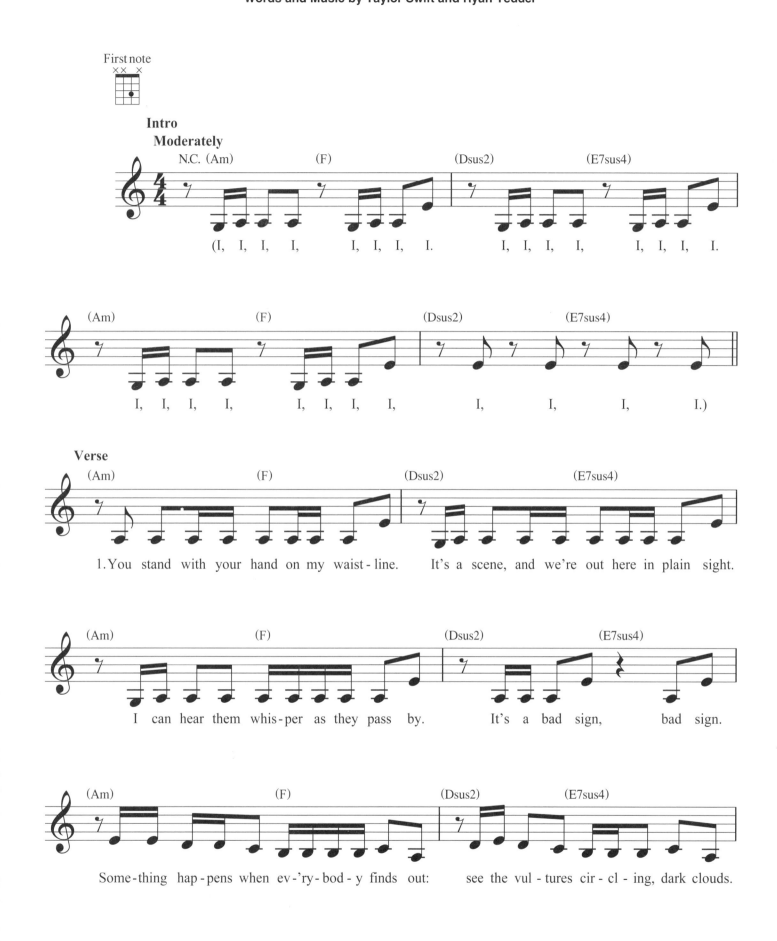

(Am) (F) (Dsus2) (E7sus4)

Love's a frag-ile lit-tle flame; it could burn out, it could burn out. __ 'Cause

Pre-Chorus

Am F Dsus2 E7sus4

they got the cag - es, they got the box - es _____ and guns.
Just grab my hand and don't ev - er drop it, _____ my love.

Am F Dsus2 N.C.

They are the hunt - ers; we are the fox - es, _____ and we run.

Chorus

C G Dm F C G

Ba - by, I know plac - es we won't be found, and they'll be

Dm F C G

chas-ing their tails __ trying to track us down. 'Cause I, _____

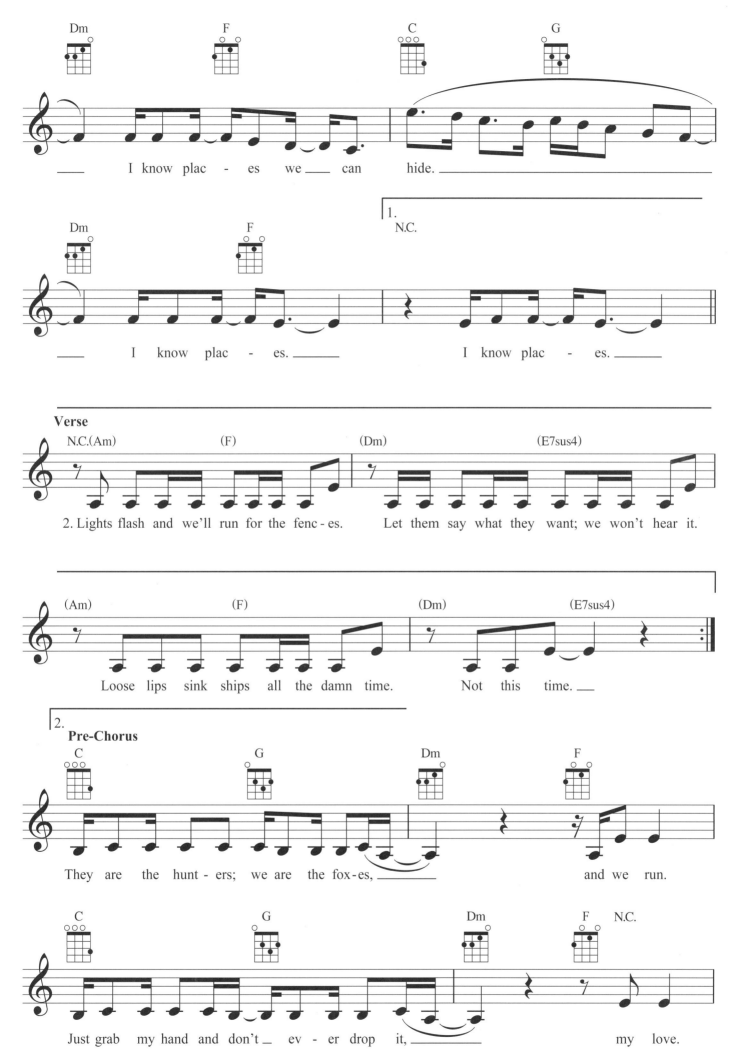

___ I know plac - es we ___ can hide. ___

1.

___ I know plac - es. ___ I know plac - es. ___

Verse

2. Lights flash and we'll run for the fenc - es. Let them say what they want; we won't hear it.

Loose lips sink ships all the damn time. Not this time. ___

2. **Pre-Chorus**

They are the hunt - ers; we are the fox - es, ___ and we run.

Just grab my hand and don't _ ev - er drop it, ___ my love.

Chorus

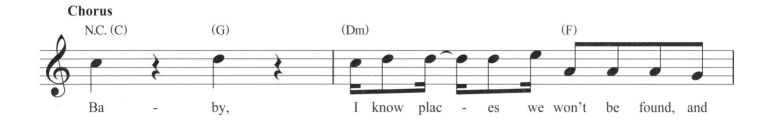

Ba - by, I know plac - es we won't be found, and

they'll be chas - ing their tails — trying to track us down. 'Cause

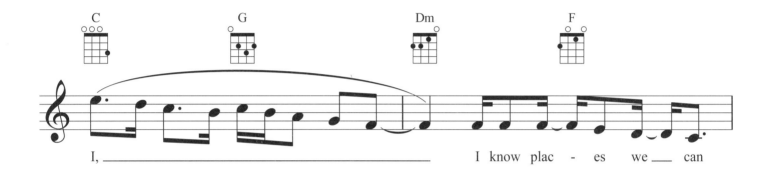

I, _____ I know plac - es we _ can

hide. _____ I know plac - es. _____

Outro-Chorus

They take _ their shots, _ but we're bul - let - proof. _____

Hide. _____ I know plac - es. _____

58

Clean

Words and Music by Taylor Swift and Imogen Heap

_____ when I could fi - nal - ly breathe. _____ And by morn - ing,

gone was an - y trace of you. I _____ think I am fi - nal - ly clean. _____

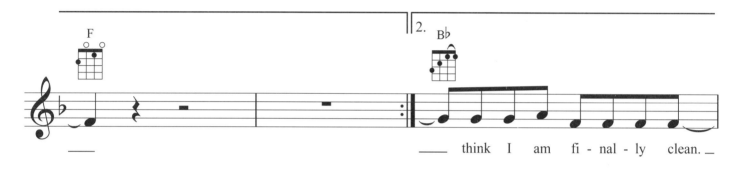

_____ think I am fi - nal - ly clean. _____

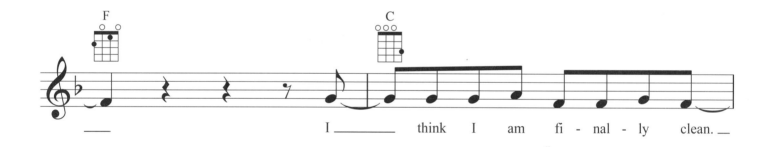

I _____ think I am fi - nal - ly clean. _____

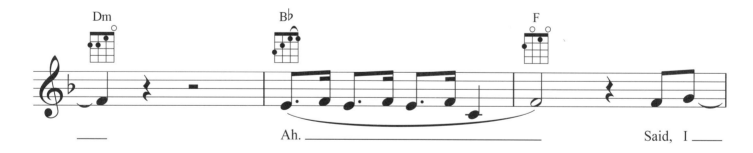

_____ Ah. _____ Said, I _____

_____ think I am fi - nal - ly clean. _____ Ah. _____